For Spacious Skies

Katharine Lee Bates and the Inspiration for "America the Beautiful"

Nancy Churnin

illustrated by **Olga Baumert**

Albert Whitman & Company
Chicago, Illinois

When Katharine Lee Bates was very young,
the Civil War raged. Some of her earliest
memories were of men trudging home in tattered blue.
Then when Abraham Lincoln was shot, Katharine's
mother wept. A hush suffocated the streets of her
village. The country's heart was ripped in two.

Katharine sat for hours, gazing at the sea. But all that the waves stirred up was empty shells, which she scooped in her apron. What could a girl growing up in the small village of Falmouth, Massachusetts, do?

No one expected much of girls in 1865. The boys she knew grew up to be fishermen or studied to become doctors or lawyers or businessmen. Girls learned to mend and cook.

Katharine didn't think that was fair.

At nine, she wrote in her diary: "Sewing is always expected of girls. Why not of boys?"

Katharine was lucky. Her widowed mother took in sewing and washing, and grew and sold vegetables to help Katharine go to school.

Some people said girls couldn't learn as well as boys.

Others said she should be thinking about marriage, not books.

Katharine didn't agree. She marveled at the power of words to make people think and feel differently. When she heard of a new college that opened just for women, she studied hard to earn a place there so she could keep writing.

At Wellesley, everyone ate the same food and lived in identical rooms. Katharine and her classmates were taught they could do anything that men could do.

But outside her school, the rich didn't mix with the poor, who worked long hours for little pay.

Women couldn't become doctors or lawyers or own businesses. They couldn't even vote.

Katharine sat for hours, gazing at Lake Waban on her college campus. What could a young woman do?

She helped establish a settlement house for immigrants and college women in Boston. She spoke up for women's suffrage and world peace. She wrote a novel, *Rose and Thorn*, about people who labored in sweatshops and struggled to care for their sick children. Her book inspired talk about how to help the poor. Katharine's words were making a difference, and she had so much more to say.

Katharine became a professor. And she kept writing.
Poems. Books. Essays.

In 1893, Katharine took a job teaching a summer class in Colorado. She traveled by train from Boston, excited to see the country on the way. In New York, she marveled at the cascading waters of Niagara Falls. In Chicago, she admired the alabaster city of the future at the World's Fair. So much beauty. So much hope.

And yet, from her work as a reformer, she knew people struggled across the country. Some groaned in dark mines; some picked crops in blistering sun; others choked for air in smoke-stained factories. As an economic depression spread dark wings across the country, people filled the streets, feeling scared and angry and alone.

On July 4, 1893, the country's birthday, Katharine sat on the train, gazing through the window. She saw the amber stalks of wheat swaying in the Kansas fields. The way they moved flooded her mind with memories of the ocean.

Suddenly she wondered: Could the people who
sail powerful waves of water and the people who tend
mighty waves of grain be more alike than we realize?

Katharine's mind might have been dancing with that idea when she arrived in Colorado and visited Pikes Peak. She rode a horse-drawn wagon up the mountain to 14,000 feet above sea level. The horse snorted and stopped.

Katharine wanted to keep going. A mule took the wagon up, up, up the final 110 feet of crumbled pink granite road to the summit.

"O beautiful!" As Katharine gazed from that height, she saw America as one unbroken country, with no walls between people.

It had been a long journey up the mountain. But Katharine was uplifted by the wonder of America. "Most glorious scenery I ever beheld," she wrote in her notebook.

The first lines of a poem rushed to her head. She wrote and rewrote in her hotel room, trying to get each word right.

Two years later, on July 4, 1895, a national magazine published Katharine's poem. People turned to one another, proudly sharing the words that described America united as a family. The poem was so popular it was published several more times, and each time Katharine revised it. By the fourth published version, she was satisfied with the poem that had come to be called "America the Beautiful."

In 1910, people started singing the poem to a melody by composer Samuel A. Ward. Now Katharine's words soared even higher.

"America the Beautiful" was the most famous poem Katharine ever wrote, but she never accepted money for it. It was her gift to America. Americans, rich and poor, men and women, from sea to shining sea, flooded her with thank-you letters.

She wrote back to every one, handwriting copies of what she jokingly called her "A the B" poem. She served coffee and cake to visitors who came to the home she shared with Katharine Coman, another professor at Wellesley. And she continued to speak up for the poor, for the rights of women, and for peace in the country and across the world.

Nine years after "America the Beautiful" became popular as a song, Congress passed the Nineteenth Amendment, which gave women the right to vote. In 1920 Katharine strode to the ballot box, filled with joy.

Katharine never did like needles and thread. But she had crafted a poem that sewed the dreams of a diverse nation together.

America still had a long way to go toward mending the differences that pushed people apart. But on the day Katharine cast her ballot alongside and equal to men, America was one stitch closer to becoming the country she knew it could be—beautiful.

America the Beautiful
Revised Version

O beautiful for spacious skies,

For amber waves of grain,

For purple mountain majesties

Above the fruited plain!

America! America!

God shed His grace on thee,

And crown thy good with brotherhood

From sea to shining sea!

O beautiful for pilgrim feet,

Whose stern, impassioned stress

A thoroughfare for freedom beat

Across the wilderness!

America! America!

God mend thine every flaw,

Confirm thy soul in self-control,

Thy liberty in law!

O beautiful for heroes proved

In liberating strife,

Who more than self their country loved,

And mercy more than life!

America! America!

May God thy gold refine

Till all success be nobleness,

And every gain divine!

O beautiful for patriot dream

That sees beyond the years

Thine alabaster cities gleam,

Undimmed by human tears!

America! America!

God shed His grace on thee,

And crown thy good with brotherhood

From sea to shining sea!

—Katharine Lee Bates

Author's Note

Katharine Lee Bates defied the expectations of her era in order to pursue her dreams and ideals.

She was born in Falmouth, Massachusetts, a few years before the beginning of the Civil War, which ended in 1865, when she was almost six. Katharine's father had died shortly after she was born. She and her three older siblings were raised by their mother, who supported Katharine's desire to study and be independent at a time when women were expected to marry and take care of the home. Katharine was in the second graduating class of Wellesley College and went on to become a professor and head of the English department there.

Katharine could be whimsical, writing fanciful works for children, including "Goody Santa Claus on a Sleigh Ride," a poem that introduced children to Mrs. Claus, in 1889. She loved having her picture taken with her collie, Hamlet, and her parrot, Polonius. She was also admired for her serious literary accomplishments. One of her earliest poems was praised by Henry Wadsworth Longfellow. Katharine was widely respected as an academic and became the first woman to write a textbook on American literature.

Additionally, Katharine was a passionate advocate for women's equality and the rights of the poor. She cofounded Denison House, a Boston settlement house that provided social services for those in need, and she spoke out for the rights of immigrants and workers.

A prolific poet, she's most famous for "America the Beautiful." After the poem was first published in 1895, people sang it to familiar tunes, including "Auld Lang Syne." In 1910, Samuel A. Ward's melody, "Materna," was published with the poem. Ward had died in 1903; he would never know how beloved his music would become. Katharine made changes to the poem and republished it in 1904 and 1911, with final changes in 1913. A national contest was held in 1926 to create new music for the poem, but in the end, the public liked Ward's "Materna" best. Although the honor of being America's national anthem was given to another song, "The Star-Spangled Banner," in 1931, many people regard "America the Beautiful" as an unofficial anthem.

Katharine had a close companionship with another professor at Wellesley, Katharine Coman, for twenty-five years. After Coman's death in 1915, Katharine dedicated a book of poems to Coman called *Yellow Clover: A Book of Remembrance*. She kept writing and advocating for women's rights and was proud when women won the right to vote in 1920. Katharine died in Wellesley, Massachusetts, on March 28, 1929. She's buried at Oak Grove Cemetery in Falmouth. She's been honored with a professorship in her name at Wellesley, an induction in the Songwriters Hall of Fame, and a plaque with the words of "America the Beautiful" at the summit of Pikes Peak.

Timeline

1859 Katharine Lee Bates is born in Falmouth, Massachusetts, on August 12.

1861 The American Civil War begins.

1865 The Civil War ends. President Abraham Lincoln is assassinated.

1880 Katharine graduates in the second class of Wellesley College in Wellesley, Massachusetts, and is honored as class president and class poet.

1885 Katharine returns to Wellesley as an instructor; in later years she becomes a professor and chair of the English department.

1889 Katharine publishes her prize-winning book, *Rose and Thorn.*

1893 Katharine visits Pikes Peak near Cascade, Colorado. The view inspires her to write lines of a poem that will eventually become "America the Beautiful."

1895 The first version of Katharine's poem is published in *The Congregationalist* with the title "America." It would be republished with changes in the *Boston Evening Transcript* in 1904 and in her poetry collection, *America the Beautiful and Other Poems*, in 1911.

1898 Katharine's book *American Literature*, the first American literature textbook written by a woman, is published.

1910 "America the Beautiful" is published with music Samuel A. Ward originally wrote for a hymn in 1882 and becomes popular as a song.

1918 On November 11, the day World War I ends, the Twenty-Sixth Infantry Division of the US Army sings "America the Beautiful" in response to the news of the armistice.

1920 The Nineteenth Amendment is ratified, enabling women to vote.

1925 Katharine retires from Wellesley but stays active as a writer and speaker.

1929 Katharine dies of pneumonia on March 28, in her home in Wellesley, Massachusetts, listening to her friend, Marion Guild, read aloud John Greenleaf Whitter's poem, "At Last." She is buried at Oak Grove Cemetery in Falmouth, the city where she was born.

Selected Sources

Bates, Katharine Lee. *Goody Santa Claus on a Sleigh Ride*. Seattle: Amazon Digital Services, 2013.

Ponder, Melinda M. *Katharine Lee Bates: From Sea to Shining Sea*. Chicago: Windy City Publishers, 2017.

Sherr, Lynn. *America the Beautiful: The Stirring True Story Behind Our Nation's Favorite Song*. New York: PublicAffairs, 2001.

Younger, Barbara. *Purple Mountain Majesties: The Story of Katharine Lee Bates and America the Beautiful*. New York: Dutton, 1998.

Quotes in the text are from Katharine Lee Bates's diary and essays. A complete source list is available at www.nancychurnin.com.

Acknowledgments

My deepest gratitude to Katharine Lee Bates's great-great-grandnieces, Katharine Lee Holland and Elizabeth Olmstead Null, for taking the time and care to read this for accuracy. I'm grateful to author Melissa M. Ponder for her notes and support; to Rebecca Goldsmith, college archivist at Wellesley College, for her help; and to Katharine Lee Bates for shining a light to our better selves. Thank you also to my wonderful editor, Wendy McClure, who made this journey a joy; to my family, for their love and encouragement; and to children everywhere. You make America beautiful.

For my boys, Ted, Sam, David, and Josh, with love and hope always for "brotherhood from sea to shining sea!"—NC

For my parents: Joanna and Daniel, love you!—OB

Library of Congress Cataloging-in-Publication data is on file with the publisher.
Text copyright © 2020 by Nancy Churnin
Illustrations copyright © 2020 by Albert Whitman & Company
Illustrations by Olga Baumert
First published in the United States of America in 2020 by Albert Whitman & Company
ISBN 978-0-8075-2530-2 (hardcover)
ISBN 978-0-8075-2529-6 (ebook)
Printed in China
10 9 8 7 6 5 4 3 2 1 HH 24 23 22 21 20 19

Design by Rick DeMonico

For more information about Albert Whitman & Company,
visit our website at www.albertwhitman.com.